Healthy Me

Eating Well

Ryan Wheatcroft   Katie Woolley

WAYLAND

First published in Great Britain in 2018 by Wayland

Copyright © Wayland, 2018

Editor: Victoria Brooker
Designer: Anthony Hannant, Little Red Ant

ISBN: 978 1 5263 0557 2

10 9 8 7 6 5 4 3 2 1

Wayland, an imprint of
Hachette Children's Group
Part of Hodder and Stoughton
Carmelite House
50 Victoria Embankment
London EC4Y 0DZ

An Hachette UK Company
www.hachette.co.uk
www.hachettechildrens.co.uk

Printed and bound in China

MIX
Paper from
responsible sources
FSC® C104740

Contents

You Are What You Eat!

Eating is something we do every day. The food you eat and the water you drink keeps you alive. Food and water help your body to think, grow, move and breathe.

Everyone needs to eat a balanced diet every day. This gives your body the nutrients it needs to stay healthy. Food can be put into food groups. You need to eat a little bit from each group to have a balanced diet.

Where Does Your Food Go?

As soon as you put food into your mouth it begins to be digested as you chew it. Digestion is the breaking down of food. Once your food enters your stomach, it mixes with acids that turn it into a thick liquid.

Mouth:
Your food mixes with saliva as you chew and swallow it.

Oesophagus:
The food moves from your mouth, down to your stomach.

Stomach:
Your food mixes with acids that help to turn it into a liquid.

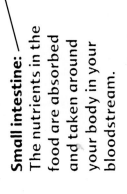

Small intestine:
The nutrients in the food are absorbed and taken around your body in your bloodstream.

Large intestine:
The parts of the food your body can't use are moved along, ready to be got rid of when you next go to the toilet!

This liquid in your stomach moves into your intestines. Your small intestine absorbs the nutrients from the food. Your large intestine leads the unused parts of your food out of your body when you go to the toilet.

What are Vitamins and Minerals?

Vitamins and minerals are substances found in food. Your body needs vitamins to work properly and to help you grow. Each vitamin does an important job, for example Vitamin C, found in fruit and vegetables, helps your skin to heal if you get a cut.

Your body uses minerals to perform different jobs, too. Calcium is a mineral that helps to build strong bones. The mineral iron, found in red meat and green vegetables, helps take oxygen from your lungs to the rest of your body.

Carbohydrates

Carbohydrates can be found in starchy foods such as bread, potatoes, cereals and pasta. Carbohydrates give your body most of its energy needs. This energy is slowly released to keep you fuller for longer.

Protein

Your body needs protein to grow, build and repair itself. It helps makes your bones strong and healthy. You get protein from food such as meat, fish, nuts, beans, seeds, eggs and cheese.

Milk and Dairy

Milk and dairy contain calcium, which helps to keep your bones and teeth healthy. Food such as cheese and yoghurt are all made from milk and dairy. Your body needs about three portions of milk and dairy every day.

Fruit and Vegetables

Your body needs at least five portions of fruit and vegetables every day. A portion of fruit or veg is about the same size as the palm of your hand. Each portion contains lots of vitamins and minerals to keep your body healthy.

Fats

Your body needs essential fats to grow, but not too much! Fatty foods give you energy, help your body absorb some vitamins and protect your nervous system.

Unsaturated fats can be good for your heart. They can be found in nuts, seeds, avocados and oily fish.

Saturated fats, found in meat, butter and cream give us energy but not many nutrients. Your body needs less of this type of fat.

Sugar

The sugar you eat is a kind of carbohydrate. Eating sugary foods can make you feel full for a while but you're missing out on important nutrients that are in healthier foods. Too much sugar is also bad for your teeth. Having sugary foods as a treat is OK as part of a balanced diet.

Water

Water helps your brain and body to function. The healthiest drinks are water and milk, as these don't contain extra sugar that can damage your teeth.

The amount of water you need depends on your age, the weather and how much exercise you do. Try to drink between 6 and 8 glasses a day.

Ready, Set, Breakfast!

Eating breakfast gives your body the energy it needs to begin the day. You'll be less tired and grumpy and be able to concentrate more when you've had something to eat.

What you eat in the morning is important. Eating foods that contain whole grain, fibre and protein such as cereals, porridge and eggs are all good for you. What is your favourite breakfast food?

Lunchtime Pit Stop

When your stomach starts to rumble during the day, your body's telling you that it's time to eat. A busy morning of exercise, learning and play will have used up the energy you got from your breakfast. It's time to refuel and stop for lunch!

A healthy lunch doesn't need to be boring!
Choosing some colourful fruit and vegetables,
your favourite sandwich filling on brown bread
and a glass of milk are all delicious ways to enjoy
a healthy lunch.

Dinner is Served!

Dinner is just as important a meal for your body as breakfast and lunch, as it's the last meal you will eat before bed. A dinner packed with healthy carbohydrates and proteins will fill you up and help you get a good night's sleep.

You can cook together in the kitchen and share stories about your day.

Sitting down for a meal at the end of the day is also chance to catch up with all your family.

Snack Attack!

Your body needs refuelling in between breakfast, lunch and dinner; especially if you have been really active. Feeling hungry in between meals can make you feel tired and grumpy, so it is a good idea to eat a healthy snack.

A piece of fruit will give you energy. You could have some raw vegetables, such as carrots and cucumber, with hummus or soft cheese. You could even make a smoothie with berries, natural yogurt and a banana.

Ditch the Junk!

Some food that is high in fat, sugar and salt but low in nutrients and vitamins is often called junk food. Crisps, chips, biscuits and fizzy drinks are all junk food. They might taste nice but it's best to have them as a treat every once in a while.

These kinds of foods give you a quick energy boost but that energy is soon used up and you'll feel tired and hungry again. If you choose something healthy instead, you'll have more energy and feel happier.

Top Tips!

Mix it up! Don't get bored from eating the same thing every day. Eating lots of different kinds of foods gives your body a variety of nutrients.

Try to eat two or three portions of food packed with protein every day. For example, you could have a tuna sandwich or baked beans and scrambled eggs.

Avoid fatty foods, especially at night. They are harder to digest and can stop you getting a good night's sleep.

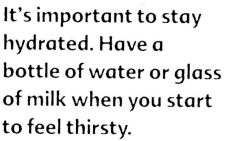

It's important to stay hydrated. Have a bottle of water or glass of milk when you start to feel thirsty.

It's great fun cooking your own food, too. Ask a grown-up if you can help make a meal.

Teachers' and Parents' Notes

This book is designed for children to begin to learn about the importance of being healthy, and the ways in which we can look after our bodies by eating well. Read the book with children either individually or in groups. Don't forget to talk about the pictures as you go.

Eating well and having a balanced diet doesn't mean eating boring food. There are lots of different kinds of foods to try. Learning to eat well is very important, as a healthy diet will help you grow, play and learn. Here are some discussion topics to encourage further thinking about eating well:

 Can you think of three reasons why it's important to eat well?

 Talk about the word 'healthy'. What do you think it means to be healthy?

 Different nutrients help keep different parts of your body healthy. What does calcium do? What does protein do?

Why are foods with lots fat and sugar bad for you?

 Talk about your favourite foods. Are they healthy or should they just be a treat?

Activities you can do:

 Use empty food packets to complete your own food plate collage.

 Have a go at making your own fruit smoothie as a healthy snack.

Further reading

Fact Cat: Healthy Eating by Izzi Howell (Wayland, 2017)
Healthy for Life: Food and Eating by Anna Claybourne (Franklin Watts, 2016)
Let's Read and Talk About Healthy Eating by Honor Head (Franklin Watts, 2014)

Glossary

bloodstream the blood circulating through the body of a person or animal

fibre a mineral found in food that helps move food through the body during the digestion process

minerals substances that help the body to grow and be healthy

nervous system a system of nerves and cells in the body that carries messages from the brain to various parts of the body

nutrients substances that help the body to grow and be healthy

portion an amount of food that is needed for one person

starchy foods foods that are high in starch are a good source of energy. Starch is a substance found in some food we eat, such as cereal, bread and potatoes.

whole grain made with, or containing, the whole, unprocessed grains of something

Index

Healthy Me — Titles in the series

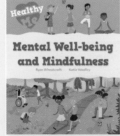